DATE DUE

1998	NOV 27	6/9/15	
FEB 16	2002		
JUN 22	JUL 18		

Looking at . . . Ornitholestes
A Dinosaur from the JURASSIC Period

THE NEW
DINOSAUR
COLLECTION

For a free color catalog describing Gareth Stevens' list of high-quality books and
multimedia programs, call 1-800-542-2595 (USA) or 1-800-461-9120 (Canada).
Gareth Stevens Publishing's Fax: (414) 225-0377.
See our catalog, too, on the World Wide Web: http://gsinc.com

Library of Congress Cataloging-in-Publication Data

Green, Tamara, 1945-
     Looking at— Ornitholestes / by Tamara Green; illustrated
by Tony Gibbons. — North American ed.
        p. cm. — (The new dinosaur collection)
     Includes index.
     Summary: Provides information about how the ornitholestes,
a small, quick carnivore that lived in North America in the Jurassic
period, may have looked and behaved.
     ISBN 0-8368-1733-8 (lib. bdg.)   7-19-97
     1. Ornitholestes—Juvenile literature.   [1. Ornitholestes.
2. Dinosaurs.] I. Gibbons, Tony, ill. II. Title. III. Series.
QE862.S3G758   1997
567.9'7—dc20   96-41852

This North American edition first published in 1997 by
Gareth Stevens Publishing
1555 North RiverCenter Drive, Suite 201
Milwaukee, Wisconsin 53212 USA

This U.S. edition © 1997 by Gareth Stevens, Inc. Created with original © 1996 by
Quartz Editorial Services, 112 Station Road, Edgware HA8 7AQ U.K.

Consultant: Dr. David Norman, director of the Sedgwick Museum of Geology,
University of Cambridge, England.

Additional artwork by Clare Heronneau.

Printed in the United States of America

1 2 3 4 5 6 7 8 9 01 00 99 98 97

Looking at . . . Ornitholestes
A Dinosaur from the JURASSIC Period

by Tamara Green

Illustrated by Tony Gibbons

THE NEW
DINOSAUR
COLLECTION

Gareth Stevens Publishing
MILWAUKEE

Contents

Introducing
Ornitholestes

So far, paleontologists — scientists who study the fossil remains of animals and plants — have only discovered one skeleton of the dinosaur **Ornitholestes** (OR-NITH-OH-LEST-EES), meaning "bird robber." Even so, quite a bit has been determined about its appearance and behavior from this single skeleton.

The answers to these questions — and many more — can all be found within the pages of this book.

Get ready to join us on a fascinating journey back in time. The voyage takes us, in text and pictures, to a time long before human beings even began to evolve . . . .

Where did **Ornitholestes** live? When did it exist? Why was it given this strange-sounding name? Was it an herbivore, or did it eat meat? Could it run fast? What made it different from other members of the family of dinosaurs to which it belonged?

Speedy

One of the dinosaurs inhabiting Earth in Late Jurassic times — about 140 million years ago — was **Ornitholestes**. It was a slim, small dinosaur that measured only about 6.5 feet (2 meters) from the end of its snout to the tip of its tail when fully grown.

Ornitholestes may not have been a giant, but it was still a carnivore. Scientists can tell this from its powerful jaws and sharp, strong teeth. Its head was small for a meat-eater, and it had a tiny bump, or crest, just above its nostrils.

An adult **Ornitholestes** was probably smaller than you are — so, by dinosaur standards, it was not very tall and certainly nowhere near the towering size of ferocious beasts such as **Tyrannosaurus rex** (TIE-RAN-OH-SAW-RUS RECKS) or long-necked **Diplodocus** (DIP-LOD-OH-KUS).

predator

No one is sure whether both male and female **Ornitholestes** would have had this bump. We can only guess that it may have been bigger in males if it was used for sexual display. Perhaps females did not have this bump at all.

Ornitholestes would certainly have needed to run at high speed in order to catch the small animals and birds that were its prey.

Scientists once thought that **Ornitholestes** was slow-moving. Now, however, they generally agree that it was fast on its feet and probably held its long tail high off the ground as it ran along.

Streamlined

Ornitholestes had a skeleton that resembles those of other *coelurosaurs* (SEA-LURE-OH-SAWRS), the family to which this Late Jurassic dinosaur belonged.

All of the coelurosaurs had slender bodies and fairly long necks.

They also had slim legs and three-toed feet, as well as long tails. These allowed the coelurosaurs to keep their balance when they ran after prey or when they had to change direction quickly. Such a tail would also have been ideal for swatting flies on a warm, muggy Late Jurassic day.

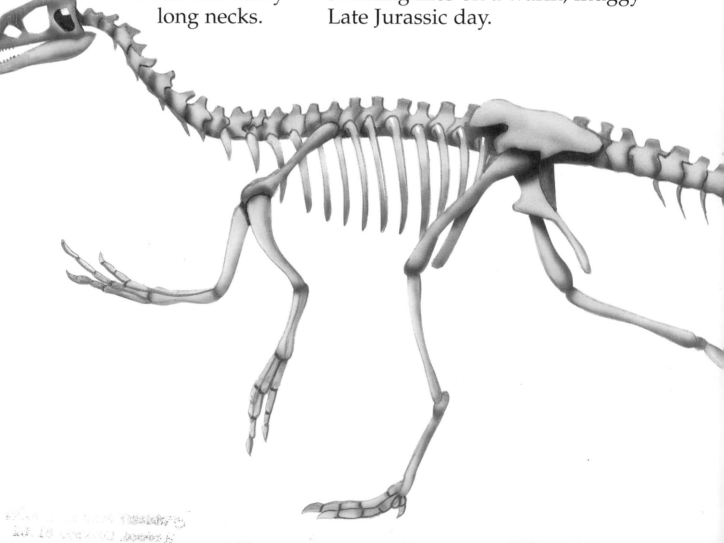

skeleton

Coelurosaurs also had three bones in their hips, each pointing in a different direction. Experts therefore refer to them as being "lizard-hipped" or *saurischians* (SAW-<u>RISK</u>-EE-ANS), to use the scientific term. In other dinosaurs — the *ornithischian* (ORN-ITH-<u>ISK</u>-EE-AN) or "bird-hipped" type — two of these bones were parallel, pointing the same way.

Members of the coelurosaur family were so much alike that scientists even confused their skeletons at first and did not realize that **Ornitholestes** differed in some ways.

Then, in 1980, almost eighty years after the bones of an **Ornitholestes** had first been discovered, a paleontologist named John Ostrom from Yale University in the United States pointed out how it probably differed from the others.

Ornitholestes did indeed have distinguishing features. Its skull was small, like the skulls of other family members, and only about 5.5 inches (13.8 centimeters) long. But Professor Ostrom noticed that **Ornitholestes** seemed to have had more teeth than its relatives, so it probably had a more powerful bite. It may also have been the only coelurosaur with a nasal horn.

Ornitholestes had longer arms than its relatives. Its hands were unique, too. On each, it had two long fingers and a shorter first finger, or thumb.

Scientists think **Ornitholestes** used this smaller finger for grasping at prey, since it could bend inward.

You can meet some of the other members of the coelurosaur family on pages 20 and 21.

Dinosaur

It all started as an idea to have some fun. Back in 1876, Henry Fairfield Osborn — a young man at the time — was laughing and joking with a friend as they dried off after a swim. As they talked, the idea came up that they should try some dinosaur hunting.

Osborn thought this would be fun even if they didn't find anything, so he agreed. Little did he realize at the time that this was to be the beginning of an important career in paleontology. He eventually became one of the world's greatest names in the field and was responsible for much of the magnificent dinosaur collection now housed in the American Museum of Natural History in New York.

detectives

Among Osborn's most famous projects were explorations at Como Bluff and Bone Cabin quarries in the state of Wyoming. Here, his team of detectives found a wealth of dinosaur fossils. In just six years, they succeeded in digging up about 75 tons of them in all.

There were so many dinosaur bones that a certain farmer, not realizing what they were, had been using them as beams and props to build a cabin. This is how the Bone Cabin quarry got its name. And it was in this quarry that the fossilized skeletal remains of **Ornitholestes** were discovered in 1900. You can see some here, under a magnifying glass.

11

Back to Late Jurassic times

Let's imagine you have built a time machine and can travel back about 150 million years at the press of a button. This fantasy journey might only take a few seconds, but you would be in for a big surprise.

Our planet looked very different in prehistoric times than it does today. There were no human beings, for example, so you are the only one around. And, of course, there are no towns or buildings at all.

Don't bother to put on a coat — you won't need one — but be sure to bring along an umbrella. The Jurassic weather forecast promises a very warm day as usual, with heavy rain.

After a bumpy landing, you find yourself at the edge of a forest that is thick with conifers, ferns, and ginkgoes.

Look! There's an **Ornitholestes**, chasing after a salamander. Now what's that curious, loud, crunching noise coming from overhead? What a fabulous sight! A lofty **Diplodocus** is browsing on a tall tree. Suddenly, though, a terrible screeching sound drowns out its chomping. Two huge, broad-winged pterosaurs have taken to the skies and are squawking a warning.

Quickly! Back to your time machine. There's not a moment to lose. An enormous **Allosaurus** (AL-OH-SAW-RUS) is approaching, and the taste of human flesh would be something new, and possibly appetizing, to this frightening carnivore.

Greedy beasts

The **Ornitholestes** were all very hungry. Another Jurassic morning had dawned, and rumbling dinosaur stomachs had to be filled.

When **Ornitholestes** was first discovered, scientists decided to give it a name meaning "bird robber." Remains found near its skeleton showed that it probably ate many different sorts of small creatures.

But this dinosaur obviously had unusual hands. They were very well suited to gripping things, and this would have helped it pick up round objects — such as eggs, perhaps.

Ornitholestes may also have been able to catch early species of birds to eat as a light meal. They may have scavenged for food, too. These small carnivores, therefore, had plenty of choices for their daily breakfast menu.

On one day in particular, two young **Ornitholestes**, already able to fend for themselves, are fighting over a lizard that looks appetizing. Two others chase a small shrew. It will take quite a few of these little animals to satisfy a growing dinosaur's appetite.

An adult male **Ornitholestes**, meanwhile, has spotted a dinosaur's nest dug into the ground. The mother has gone off to feed. Greedily, it grasps an egg and gobbles it up. Drooling, it notices that there are more where that came from.

Many creatures in the forest had to be watchful when even small predators like **Ornitholestes** were on the prowl for a meal.

A dinosaur success story

Life on Earth began about 3 billion years ago with tiny, single-celled creatures. A huge span of time passed before dinosaurs eventually evolved about 200 million years ago, as shown at the top of this time ribbon.

Not all dinosaurs lived at the same time. Some species would die out, and other species would then evolve. But, in total, dinosaurs were around on our planet for about 160 million years.

In comparison, human beings have only been in existence for a very short while — just 100,000 years. Dinosaurs ruled the world, therefore, for more than fifty times as long. That's why the boy at the end of the time ribbon takes up such a small space.

How, then, did dinosaurs survive for so long? Scientists think one reason was that they adapted to their environment. Some dinosaurs were herbivores; others were carnivores. So there would have been enough food for them all. They were also well-suited to living on land and had tough skins. Even baby dinosaurs had a good chance of survival because they hatched from hard-shelled eggs that protected them while they were developing.

Dinosaur National

By 1915, many superb skeletons of herbivores such as **Diplodocus**, **Apatosaurus** (A-<u>PAT</u>-OH-<u>SAW</u>-RUS), and **Stegosaurus** (<u>STEG</u>-OH-<u>SAW</u>-RUS), as well as carnivores like **Allosaurus** had been discovered in the area around the town of Vernal in northeastern Utah.

Because of these discoveries by such great dinosaur hunters as Earl Douglass, President Woodrow Wilson of the United States decided that the area should be protected by American law. Also, in recognition of all the discoveries that had been made in the region, the entire area, comprising 80 acres (32 hectares), was named Dinosaur National Monument.

The quarry there contains one of the largest deposits of dinosaur remains to have been found anywhere in the world. There is even a working museum so visitors can see the skeletons as they are exposed.

Most special about Dinosaur National Monument is the fact that remains of almost all the different dinosaurs from Late Jurassic times have been found there.

In this illustration, you can see an early 20th-century paleontologist working in the quarry.

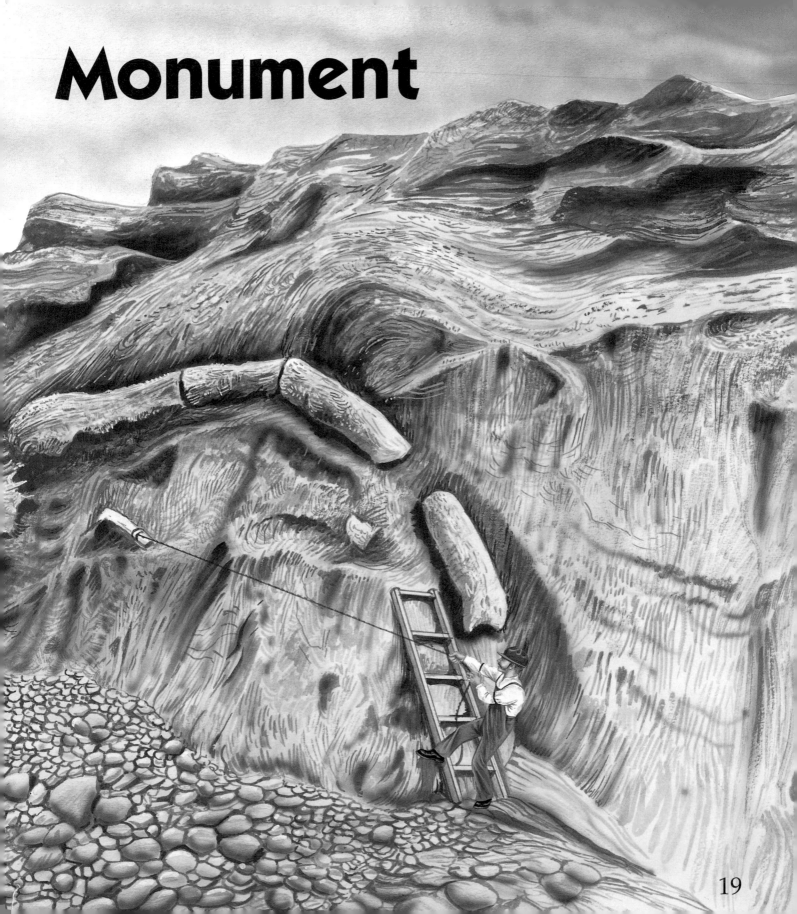

Monument

Dinosaurs belonging to this family are called *coelurosaurs*, meaning "hollow-tailed reptiles," because their tail bones seem to have been very lightweight and spongy. **Ornitholestes** (1) and all the coelurosaurs were small by dinosaur standards; even the largest of them were not very tall. Not many coelurosaur fossils have been found. But paleontologists still know a lot about this family.

Kakuru (KAK-OO-ROO) (2), for example, with a name meaning "rainbow serpent," was first discovered in South Australia. It lived in Early Cretaceous times, about 135 million years ago, so it lived later than **Ornitholestes**. About 8 feet (2.4 m) long, it would have looked and behaved much like **Ornitholestes**, except that, like other coelurosaurs, it probably had no head crest of any sort.

1

2

family

Far smaller — not much bigger than a chicken, in fact — was **Compsognathus** (COMP-SOG-<u>NATH</u>-US) (**3**). It has a name meaning "pretty jaw" and was a speedy, two-legged carnivorous dinosaur from Late Jurassic Europe.

Another larger coelurosaur dates from Triassic times, before **Ornitholestes** had even evolved. This was **Coelophysis** (SEEL-OH-<u>FI</u>-SIS) (**4**). It was about 10 feet (3 m) long and seems to have had a fourth finger, but no thumb. Its bones were first discovered at a place called Ghost Ranch in Texas. Scientists think **Coelophysis** may have been a cannibal because the bones of smaller **Coelophysis** skeletons were found inside the remains.

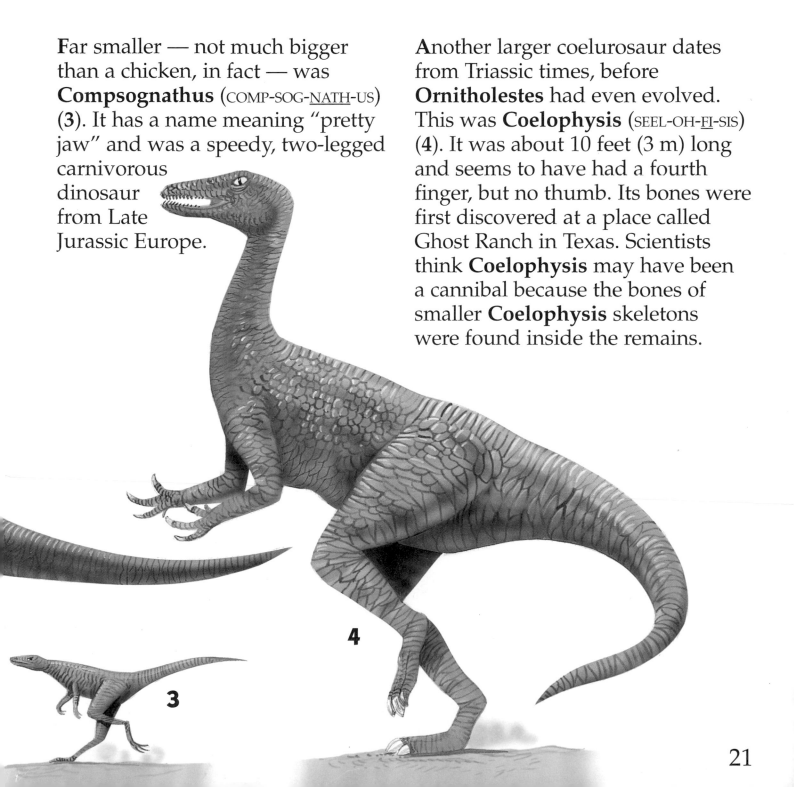

4

3

Ornitholestes data

Dinosaurs were not all massive. In fact, **Ornitholestes** probably had footprints that were about the size of yours. These prints would only have three toes, however, although there was a tiny extra toe that turned backward at the ankle and did not touch the ground.

Agile hunter

As well as its small, light feet and slim limbs, **Ornitholestes** had another feature that made it speedy.

Long, tapering tail

Ornitholestes's tail was longer than the rest of its body. And the bony rods inside the tail kept its tail stiff as the dinosaur ran.

Nasal crest

The tiny bump, or crest, on **Ornitholestes**'s snout may have given it a more powerful appearance.

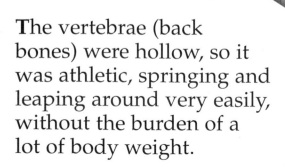

The vertebrae (back bones) were hollow, so it was athletic, springing and leaping around very easily, without the burden of a lot of body weight.

Grasping hands

Ornitholestes had a thumb but only two other, longer fingers on each hand. But this did not matter because, just as *our* thumbs help us grasp things, so **Ornitholestes** also used its thumbs for gripping. It would have been very difficult for it to hold on to anything securely without these smaller, flexible digits.

Nasty bite

Ornitholestes's teeth were so strong that any creature falling victim to its jaws must have writhed in pain and wriggled like crazy to escape. Mealtimes were probably very noisy in the Jurassic world. Herbivores chomped loudly on plants, and carnivores roared as they went for the kill, while their unfortunate prey yelped in agony as the meat-eaters' razor-sharp teeth punctured their flesh.

GLOSSARY

carnivores — meat-eating animals.

conifers — woody shrubs or trees that bear their seeds in cones.

crest — a growth on top of an animal's head.

evolve — to change shape or develop gradually over a long period of time.

ginkgoes — trees with showy, fan-shaped leaves and yellow fruit.

herbivores — plant-eating animals.

paleontologists — scientists who study the remains of plants and animals that lived millions of years ago.

predators — animals that kill other animals for food.

prey — animals that are killed for food by other animals.

quarry — a place where stone, marble, or fossils are excavated, or dug up, from the ground.

remains — a skeleton, bones, or dead body.

scavenge — to eat the leftovers or carcasses of other animals.

INDEX